Vyt Bakaitis
No More Time

SPUYTEN DUYVIL
New York City

ISBN 978-1-963908-71-8

Library of Congress Control Number: 2025940458

Contents

Timespan

When something inside dies
is it weariness merely, or some
outgrowth of time's leisurely erasure?

Today simply appears to be as it is
reality gets blurred just so
much as the eye easily distracted

The few hours we shared in sunlight
all ours and not to be forgotten
but when they ask what will we tell them?

Its stem the laugh grows a kiss to share
an engulfed labyrinth we intend to bare
a searching tongue even as we speak

You You You look great
You be good. See you then
with a sunset to keep our eyes on

There'll be a lot of explaining to do
while you babble on in French
I'll press on in mock Sanskrit

Did one of us just say Babylon?
That's a laugh a kiss can grow out of
yours or mine to be shared in

She said Babel because that
was the only excuse she had
to join in the laughter

We have all the time
the hours are ours while
your radiant beauty outshines the sun

(A foreground in passing
from moment to emotion
confirmed but left unresolved

From an individual
to social expansion
is one justification

How to bring on
belief for a basic
concept of justice

That cults and all
religious point The Way
for each one to find "a way"

Wayward via extremism
here and right now their own
from a hospital bed

There must be some mistake
just to lie here and think
only about getting out

Uncertain ticker or
as a friend's email
is bound to remind me

Emotion is
all it is
in passing)

On A Nada Cantata for 11 March 06

Along with the author, appearing as performers:

     Gintare Bukauskas

     Rolandas Andrijauskas

     Jurate Kajokaite

     Larry Miller

     Greg Masters

     Rasa Pranckunaite

Fluxus is nothing if not current.

One may aim to advance its flow from an established basis in plain inanity to an equally mindless, mildly provocative sophomoric stammer.

But whatever line it is made to follow, there is never a trend.

The Nada Cantata for 11 March 06

[*first speaker, after harsh whistle:*]
STOP THE SHOW.
WE'RE HERE TO CLOSE THE OPENING.

[*all together, sing: to the tune of* "Glory glory hallelujah"]
we're in love with George Maciunas
even though he's nothing to us
and we honor Jonas Mekas
for bringing him around

[*female speaker, solo:*]
mylime mes George Mačiūną
kirsime jam po bizūną
nors jis iškeliavo dūmais
mes taikom prisivyt
šiaip taip net atgaivint

[*male speaker, solo:*]
gerbiame ir Joną Meką
kad negrimstų jis į peklą
rišim virvę jam per kaklą
arčiau rojaus pritaikyt
ir šventai taip išlaikyt

[*first speaker:*]
so we honor Jonas Mekas
though he never really asked us
to join the underground
for bringing George around

[*all together sing:*]
we're in love with George Maciunas
even though he's nothing to us
now having ventured into grief
let's heave a sigh of deep relief

[*male speaker:*]
Kelsim jį ant plataus samčio
virš gilios mirties balos
[female speaker]
Išlaikysim taip per amžius
gyvą kaip ankščiaus

[*second speaker:*]
So let's honor George Maciunas
for the work he quit as soon as
it got done for surely by design
he left his work unsigned

[*third speaker:*]
And the wonder of it is
so much plainly wasn't his
no one would consider theft
such collaboration left

[*fourth speaker:*]
Overall as all items align
Gratitude! clearly the sign

[*fifth speaker:*]
What we know of him is now
simply hearsay but enough
to cram archives with the stuff

[*all together:*]
That some of us
know it really was
due to George's stammered laugh

[*female speaker, solo, sadly:*]
No George Maciunas
[*first male speaker, solo, sadly:*]
No George Maciunas
[*second male, solo, sadly:*]
No George Maciunas

[*all together, buoyant & loud:*]
IS NOT DEAD

POEM FOR THE DEAD

If the dead would only speak to us
When all the lights are out
And we've paced off all the trails
It takes to wear down doubt

They could sneak up to say
What went wrong in the way
They left us or simply sign in
With the nudge of a grin

Let them not catch us off guard
When we're working too hard
To share with the living
The few breaks we've been given

Happier now than we've been
Though we hear them close in
For no particular reason
On no occasion or season

Of course they don't have to exist, no
Not even for the brusque imposition
Of a close to overwhelming relation
They may sometimes insist on

While their vigilance may be astounding
Their presence is kept a neighborly trust
When day dawns with nothing to give us
They're the ones we'll choose to go on living with

FULL FATHOM FIVE

The roundtrip
an aggrieved
philosopher
once proposed
stems from suffering

That must have
touched me in reverse
my first conscious thought
I was just short of five
moved me to uncover the past

A lifetime before my birth showed
no more clear sign than that
I'd been there before

POSTSCRIPT

Now we count days
          soon the hours
drift into gear
          numb and absurd
the little we know
          will grow less
no lingering thought
          will have any appeal
flecks of memory for some
          who may show up
for the memorial
          so the notion of trust
evaporates with grief

A Small Reminder

Once in the South of France
when Helen got to the beach
she dropped to her knees and
stayed that way a while, thinking

Her husband then said: What
do you think he's doing
over there with the sand?

She looked and saw
Picasso squatting and knew
just what he was up to

But being too bashful
she stayed put and kept
her poise until

The great artist had left
then she jumped up and
ran over for a close look

C'est moi! she exclaimed
C'est vrai, her husband agreed
Before the tide washed it away

But for the rest of her life
the image was never erased
from her mind

WARTIME CHILDREN'S SONG

You, fox!
You
That stole the goose from us
Give 'er back, right now.
Give 'er back, at once.
Otherwise
We'll let the hunter
Shoot you with his gun.

Post Mort

Hey! Hey!
What's ahead?
I've praised the dead,
Earned my bread,
Paid my debts
And made my bed.
Now I'll just see what
Ever Byron may have
Had to say instead.

Want & Wait

The way you toss the word away
Are you not forgetting where it went
Away is a long way from today even when
Near here is having you nowhere to hold on to

There's no way of saying "had enough"
When the only way is to wait it through
Even though I break up every time
You leave like there's nowhere to go
Should I track your ashes on the trail

Hello Young Lovers

you're right on time, a target that suits you too, that's not
                                                    been displaced
though it's wild in America, exoskeletal and macromolecular
this cusp of a Presidentiad, no choice without a clue

and you're right to close your eyes, the moon's X-rated neon
chameleon's a target that has been displaced, though too far
off to tell: is it hollow, or does light shine clear through?

and follow your own closed notions of space, exploring the gamey
nonsense of pre-nuptial declaration, sham cloister elaborations on
delights & trepidations, to the test of distraction, all the rest

by sweat-ducts climb up on a prime drain-on-the-valley cleavage
a heart's cannonade, rock and shudder at the radio's tombstone

to the evident delight of the stars

A Silence White

We stood in Venice
down a narrow lane
across from the house
where Pound once lived
a sign by the door said RUDGE

Just then
a feather fell
swirled its descent
to land at our feet
on the small stoop
where we stood
and looked

It was so small
all white
we took as a sign
of the silence and
when we looked up
the sun was higher

We left it there
and kept the look
ingrained in our
memory still

With Blake, in London

for William Benton

Bad poems
more than enough
too soon to drown in

(breath's refrain a bluff)

(wind's huff)

2.

I WILL MAKE THIS NEWSPAPER MINE
LEAD-LINED WINDOWS AND ALL
KINDS OF CRUD TO FIT AND FILL
TO THE SKY-HIGH MARGINS

It could be that, according to Blake
we're surely obliged
to start with a fart
inarticulate to oblivion

3.

There are a few translations in the book, in halting versions,
        mute imitations,
fluid insinuations, fakes or frustrations. No stray paradoxes,
        strict adaptations.
No paradigms, or paraphrases. At best, traces of reluctant
        agitation. All
those voices.

4.

Now the shark has set his teeth
these he'll flash right in your face

INCIDENTAL

and turn each time
birds say your name

and come calling

WHEREVER

When you dream of someone
all too far away, you'd never
hear the voice they spoke in
though the image stays

How I think of Nanno now
is a blur of golden light
the shimmer of pure day
I cannot hold on to

Delights are few where memory
Dwells though always out of reach
Their particulars will continue
to teach and guide us to pursue

Nanno's name one banner
brightens early morning

Old Time SOS

There's one girl in that bar I didn't get to know.
She'd smiled, engagingly.
"Next time we meet no longer strangers"
I said the line
straight from a Japanese phrasebook.

I never saw her again.
The next day I shipped out.

Distressing, the way her face stuck
to each cobblestone, in all the harbors
my ship touched en route.

A. M. / P. M.

Shadows close down and stick
        close
              down
                     and
                           stick

                         break
                  to
           shade
       trips
Window trips shade to break

HOLDERLIN: SURVIVING FRAGMENTS
from the German

Little to go on, but lots of enthusiasm
Is what we're stuck with

Once the glory eyes delight in gives out for lack of human
Acclaim, the trails unshaded with the trees bare,
And riches a child's eyes gawked at now grown
More vigorous
In ruin

O Island of Light

SIMULTANEITY IS THE KEY

Like massive trucks that whine by
Moving too fast on the highway
Swept away on a slim verge
One election-year summer
Flat out of gas

Wartime Hearsay

If a snowdrop falls
and settles it stays
where it belongs
but not for long.

*

Take the sand
one element you don't
need to break down
to any less than dust.

Besides
other than smoke and blood
your oil spills and burns
what have you got?

On The Town

We'll squander
everything we share.
That accounts for
the prevalence of noise.

The children we were
did not grow up here,
one guess that did
leave us wondering.

Statistics compress
to an inscrutable static.
Each code, once cracked,
gets trashed.

Who drives anymore?

HERE'S HOPING

Let's hope that with you
I'm among the happy few
to keep my thoughts warm
while still thinking of home

POSTMARKED, BACK WHEN

O to be a quarter
on the open market!
sings the dime in my pocket,
still only 10¢.

2

Your hand in mine is not warm,
the dime in my coat pocket
just warm enough
that I don't know it's there
until I touch it. Then it is
welcome, the fingers touching it
warm too. I kiss your hand,
Starting at the fingertips.

3

I love you
I have decided
I love you
I'm not so sure
I love you
I change my mind

4

We sit on a rock.
I rub
My palm on the rock's
cool hide. It
will always be stone.

5

If there were two of you
I'd know just what to do,
I suppose. As it is, when I ask
what's the matter, you really
blow up, yelling at me to stop
following you!

My head
weighs 100 lbs, at least.
The sidewalk comes closer and closer.
Full of windows, one
on top of another,
that I can't see in.

I am going to follow you.
I won't leave you alone.
And everything is going to be different.

I've got a dime.
Not even a phonecall!

6

Slowly it comes to me, in a story. A horse, smarting,
tosses its head up and down, a definite yes; then, rearing,
snorts; and the air is charged with alternatives. Then the
horse, a stallion, gallops off down the path. Leaving the
air heavy all around, the rider light on its back.

When I open my eyes, you are not the same. You are
different. And far away.

Late Poem, before It Gets Lost

It was good to see you as you are
       a natural beauty even for the gray in your hair your nose
       snub your rustic complection your laughter fresh air

It was good to see you as I should have known you
       before long as too good to last too strong

It was good to see you though you aren't
       here and I can't hope to
       ever again hear you

It was so good to see you but I'm not
       saying goodbye
       not just yet

JUNE

Plain-spun by ordinary daylight
The month to show off your tresses
Now a bright glow of golden curls
Abundantly frames your smile

A stunning silence
Seals my breath

Mute chords of desire
My ribs imprison
Each heartbeat plunders

The reach of my joy
Fails to enliven
The moment I stand

Framed in your glance
I'm not alone entranced

WHILE WAITING FOR AN ECLIPSE

Sunlight at play on water is the faintest of memories to behold.

We all stood around and long before the fire died down night deepened
and aligned itself unto the ashes.

My mind is on something else but I can't think of a name for it.

Alone as I am in the garden I know Eve just has to show up, since I have
the name for her already.

As for individual happiness it's the ratio of what you feel to what you see
or hear or taste or touch all stripped to an abstraction almost
before you know it.

A kiss is awkward as the itch in each embrace.

One blossom falling is like a dozen apples that never landed from
the same tree.

It was a miracle for me to know you, since no other human hand can
reach me now, not anymore.

One word doesn't fit the small plaque at the top of the cross, but could it
be Acropolis or Apocalypse or simply Agora?

I knew I couldn't read Dante by that light, so I let it flicker and stepped
out for a quick smoke.

Give me a drink with a touch of the brine and I'll launch a ship packed
for the cruise.

Even for those closest to him, Rilke couldn't contribute much
                                                    to any friendship,
always telling them as a show of concern that he'd reach them
across the ages, when they'd actually known him only a day or two.

After we entered a city we'd just captured we wouldn't give these
strangers any reprieve, though not one of their screams was anonymous,
and we left them done in as we first imagined we'd find them.

Aim the nail between my toes, a dream I had once still awaits its fulfilment.

Borderline Blues

The way I figured it was way out of control
The sky was darker than my coffee could hold
In a way I was sorry but it was too late to wait
The bullfrogs were belching to eat from my plate

A weight on my palate kept the dream delayed
Your pain was as quiet as the morning aged
And the paper slipped sideways to spill
All across our linoleum floor
If it wasn't paid for what was
The war news for

I saw a crowned head
Lie down by the bed
I knew no more news
Except I wasn't dead

My pictures were hungry
For slick leaded frames
I felt I was done for
When lust licked the flames

I knew for a fact
The nighttime was black
Nothing more to sideline
For a new second act

Acumen

Take the outer highway
       to go beyond Le Travail
But avoid the half-sunk boardwalk
       on the far-out frog pond of Despond
When you get à droite de l'Arc de Trump
       don't leave a scratch on le tomb'
And au-delà du rappel by way of thanks
       they won't reward you en francs
When you make your move à la demande
       that they hold a table to your command
Pour résoudre le erratique tom-foolery
       and désamorcer un différend boiteux
You'd think you were facing some jerk
       straight from the crew of le Cirque
And to skirt the Despond Reservoir
       go right on past un profonde désespoir
For the blest objectif finale is to find joie incarnée
       despite many ways to have gone astray
Seigneur let all the voices say
       light our lamp every day

NOTARY

How'll we
ever know so
you stand with two knives
one in each hand
to define genocide
though it could be a murder
of buddies for sure
once it's done
not to bother
it's like one to another
let's not forget the tall one
once stood by a waterfall
artificially constructed
robotic oversight
will not stop the blood flow
what could be on your hands
never too late
you must join in
the welcome we shout
to call you into a dwindling
procession to receive the Beast
speaks only in afterthoughts
understandably in memory
language independent of
experience as usual
far away and as if
for always

Borderline Link

He never crossed the line
Till he was double-crossed
Before he got there one of us
Got hauled off to slave labor
The camp we only heard about
Where high blood pressure
Felled him although he was one
Who survived having lost an eye
But that was later when he tried
Suicide before his wife grabbed
The gun away from him after
He'd collapsed and she had to
Lead him around like a dummy
By the hand and they kept
Bumping into each other like
A dance when you can't
Even hear the music

FOR MATTHEW SHEPHARD

to his memory (1976–1998)

Looking, according to the news, for love
had to be real, no less, and yet the fuse
or truce, for you, Matthew Shepard, you

wouldn't have looked at twice for
the experience, unless his was a face
held interest for a note of passing joy

in that tanktown, its brief visual imprint
individual detail indistinct so your mind
retains only the young smile

straight from last year's yearbook
now we found you alive but alone
a blind cover of night the killers
took off in with
all the light
gone from your life
to be unrecovered

the killers gone
under cover of night
your life from the light
as dawn settled on you
though there were still
traces of pain your tears
tracked in the stiffened blood
Jesus

it was too late
when we first heard
about you
and a cry for help
your last breath
Jesus

COUNTDOWN

Now we count days, soon the hours will
drift into gear, numb and meaningless
the little we know will grow less

No lingering thought will have
any more appeal
flecks of memory for some
who may dare to show up
for the memorial

All notions of trust evaporate with grief

And in time the more we talk
the longer our conversation
drifts to dredge up what
we can't always recover

What we feel is all that lasts
when the thunder rolls in
it's a passing phenomenon

Time's crimping tally
won't stop our rally

FUNERAL NOTES

I like the way they'd ring the old bell
whenever somebody died
Dull. Clanging. Monotonous

It broke the silence to pieces
yet there was a rhythm there
that somehow held you & kept
you focused enough to keep up
with the pace all the way to
the cemetery gate

Now you just get in a car
& if you don't get lost following
on a highway alive with
more important noise
ride it out in company &
get there & get it over with & let
some of the real silence sink in
before you turn back, then
if it's bleak, it will get bleaker
when you get back, and later
believe me, I've been there

A Look Ahead In Retrospect

Say what you will but whatever the anguished prospect you
came out of I know where I stand for the moment though the
inner landscape refuses to bloom.

Here the wind flattens everything to the ground already leveled
so it's cast and raised above a tarred gravel with the prospect
blocked and reciprocal caves to left and right each one arched
like a willing ear but deaf to the howling inside the hollow still
echoes like a buffered window shuttered flat black not even the
blind can see through.

Otherwise I'd have nothing to say.

HÖLDERLIN: (SONG OF FATE, FROM HYPERION)
from the German

You have it easy up there,
Happy as homebodies strolling in glory,
While sparkling perfect mild gusts
Stir you, the way
One woman plays harp with the skill
To touch holy strings.

Free of fate as babies in sleep,
Heaven's inmates inhale such bliss,
With each soul
At a fresh modest blush, for
Ever on verge
Of flowering,
Their eyes in a happy trance
Fix on a quiet
Clarity always.

But we never get to
Stay any place all that safe.
Through breakups, through failures,
Humans keep suffering
Blindly, one hour to
The next and over
Like water sent crashing
From rockledge to rockledge
All year, and vanish no one knows where.

Hölderlin: Untitled Fragment

from the German

If from the distance that we're apart
I'm someone you still recognize and our past,
O sharer in my sorrows,
Still points to something you value,

Say of this friend how she still waits for you,
Whether in gardens where we'd found
Each other after a dark unsettling phase,
Or here beside streams of the sacred primal world.

I need to say there was something to value
In your glances, the times you delighted
In looking off around you, always
A person locked inside your dark

Expression. Or while the hours flowed off, how quietly
My soul endured the truth of being
Made to stay away from you.
Yes, I did admit I was the one for you.

It really is true, the way you want to bring
By writing all that you know, in letters
To my memory, is what I go through too,
In saying over all that happened.

Was it spring or summer the sweet singing
Nightingale lived among birds not far
Away in the foliage, where the trees
Enclosed us in their full fragrance?

Low brush, and sand along clear paths
We stepped on, the hyacinth
Or tulip, violet or carnation,
Made jollier and prettier.

With ivy green on walls and fences, a spirited
Green shade was in the vaulted promenades, the many
Evenings and mornings we went there,
With much to talk over and happy to look at each other.

In my arms the young man came to,
The one left back now, in from fields
He pointed out to me with a deep sadness,
Yet the names of unusual sites

He'd retain, along with all flowering
Beauty from happy settings I also value
Greatly as the landscape of home,
Or the concealment of a high vantage

Anyone can scan the sea from, though
No one wants to be there. Let be, and think
Back to her who still is delighted that
Enchanting day did cast its spell on us,

Starting with the promise or handclasp
That made us one. O miserable me,
Those were lovely days, even though
A twilight of grief did ensue.

You are so alone in the beautiful world
You stay with me always, my love, only
You don't know it

For Adina K.

One glance the midnight bells
Chime lost desires that ever
Glow in your eyes a dawn
Their deepest dark beauty
I so aspired to now divine

Truth is what it takes to heal
And marshal the rare moment
Time's monument its testament
Your eyebrows a nighttime sign

Nor will I die unaware of
The sheer cost memory takes
Beyond each measure of reason

Wherever you've gone
Your eyes will shine on

2

Your smile may yet be gleaming
Despite its stern intent dismiss
The solid meaning I've sent
To let a dove sit on your lips
With both of its wings spread

I'll not take it for granted
If you discard my claim
To let me address you frankly
More times than heartbeats can

Though I might break the silence
Surrounding us once you're gone
My regret if you don't answer
Will decline to settle in doom
But find no dark is its home

3

I dare not go so far
     and say
The clock forbids whatever gay
       array
You may yet surprise us in on any
        given day
And keep eyes open long enough
       to pray
So the dream we had won't slip
      away
And ruin our chance to run
     astray
Then dance in the darkened
      cabaret
Even a misstep won't
    betray
Or fail to heighten
    our soirée
We'll let the stars show us
     the way
Where we've never yet been
      not today
Together or alone to run
     and play
Let our compass beam
    the ray
To let us pass or stay

No Place to Start

Impressed by a generous wash of light to warm us
even before a single voice had unleashed its decibels

Now the outrage simmers though it won't bubble the tar

If only those clamoring for their redemption
were likely to be hauled off to heaven
the ones scrambled to the rooftop and found the last depart
on choppers beyond their reach so all failed to get on board

What is the meaning of this is infinity
just an idle conceit of universal immunity

We are beaten down with a fine lasting grind
as from first to last so from birth unto death

What we saw ahead where the sky was sealed
the ground wound down in smoke rings all
around to a wind-whipped shroud
one shot or more and we're gone

Let's leave you to guess what comes next
for the least expense play it smart
save your breath

Lines before License

This is no place to say I have triangulated sorrow
Though the day-to-day is accute and spendthrift me
                              has relinquished
Another full nightly quota before the axe lobs in

So settle down
Retract your rage and let me simmer

JOSEPH BRODSKY IN MEMORY

died January 28, 1996

Tongue goes slack
so gravity drops
and the heart stops
like clockwork

What's left to assess
at what final cost reputation
grows or dims as any departure
may be said to snuff bliss
all the photos have missed

No more scowl when
the frown's gone bankrupt

Now winter's a NY state of the art
where the new year's stripped severity
kept the whole Northeast in a raw
deep freeze well into late January

At the tip of Liberty's harbor
the homeless feed smoldering drums
unwary beacons to scare away
truants and tourists

Cars flail by wheezing
to start their engines
if only you could be here
to see the moon
plumb red O Joseph
a Revelation as never before

One hell of a chill we live in
as our century glides to its close
fueling overblown wars
with no one eager to say
the coldest most terrible chill
suits poets best to die

Though it let you escape
and you died on your feet
like a stalled barge
your much acclaimed poems
stay charged this side of the Styx
awaiting "their proper translation into English"

That winter's diamond-hard
accumulated crust won't crack
though we keep hammering verses

All too smug you called them
wrong start to finish but not to end
where you began to take on

A new language
recovering from
its universal collapse into jittery panic

Now the highway's hum lifts into a keen
while you settle down and dream
a dream beyond exile

By Hart Crane's stranded harp
tossed ashore with no perceptible sea-din
with Whitman on watch where Wystan kept house

Mnemosyne takes cover
                            staring off

Where the needle stands rigid
with accelerator floored God knows
we won't be goaded to glory
you'll step up to strike a dandified pose
from the lip of the stage

Go on tell the Court what new
language do you Joseph take on
almost by default
from a tortured imagination
cleared past happenstance
the glitzy awards draped with crape

Hopefully your art pursued
the dream of another star
more a metaphysical abstract
than Malevich was forced to face up to
the plain fact of it simply there

2

Let legend keep him the man he was
once chopped wood hard as he could
whole cord in Russian cold would
be more than any even he should
though officials stated it was all
for the common communal good

And did judgment dawn on him?
Those against him
didn't do him in
while the stack stood to his chin

They told him to stop
but he never just stood
axe in hand
          and
kept on chopping
there was no stopping
him from his chopping
and stacking
till beside him stood
a whole cord of wood

No loss can appraise
at what final cost
reputation grows dim

Let legend embalm
the proud exile he was
while his poems live on

A shell washed ashore
will still keep its deep
perpetual sea-din

3

A prisoner once
ordered to cut wood
as a woodcutter should

Hard as you could
hacked at Arctic
East Russian logs

A whole cord in dull cold
much more than they
told you you should

But there you stood
in front of the cut you'd
stacked for your own good

And did the judgment bring gain?
Those against you
couldn't do you in

Though the stack stood to your chin
you kept on chopping
they told you to stop

but you never just stood
axe in hand
                and
kept on just because

till beside you stood
a whole cord of wood

That plus official dismay
quickly got you banished

But on your way to the US of A
you got strong support from

Auden and poets who hardly
knew any of your work

4

Late January in New York
a state-of-the-art winter
set its seal on the poet's breath

So any last departure
may be said to snuff bliss
the eulogists seem to miss

If only you could be here to hear
and see the moon
plumb red O Joseph
a Revelation as never before

This persistent cold-front
one hell of a chill to dive into
now our century glides to its close

We fuel overblown wars
with no one eager to say
the coldest most terrible chill
holds bitterness more terrible
suits poets best to die

While winter's diamond-hard
accumulated crust won't crack
though we keep hammering verses

You called them all wrong
start to finish but to no end
while you began to take on

A new language recovering from
our universal collapse
into a lingering panic

Where the needle stands rigid
with accelerator floored God knows
we won't be goaded to glory

You'll step up to strike a dandified pose
from the lip of the stage

Mnemosyne takes over
                          staring off

5

Sad to see not that you could
or would be allowed to
but there you stood
in a darkening wood
before the stack you'd stacked
for your own good

And did the judgment bring you justice?

As exiles are never blind
to any future opportunity
your poems survive
redeeming doggerel
by sheer force of will

Such acclaimed poems
stay charged this side of the Styx
awaiting their righteous translation

That winter's diamond-hard
accumulated crust won't crack
though we keep hammering verses

All too smug you called them
wrong start to finish but not to end
where you began to take on

A new language
recovering from
its universal collapse
into jittery panic

By Hart Crane's stranded harp
tossed ashore with no perceptible sea-din
Whitman on watch where Wystan kept house

Now the highway's hum lifts into a keen
while you settle down and dream
a dream beyond exile

Absently groping for a cigarette
though there's nothing more
in the right-hand pocket
now there's no face to focus
as in Avedon's portraits

Caught as we are
between Venus and Mars
everloving bosom and metalclad chest

Tongue goes slack
gravity drops
the heart stops
like clockwork

Joseph, we'll watch for your star

In the Pines

We're talking tomorrow, where the sun
Shines unobstructed, and the view
Stays "to try men's souls"

Just who is this dada idiot "You said it!"
Pure crystaline, under fire

Now the sky won't open on the door
To nowhere not evermore "Honey,

I junked the kids!" across two counties with
Fireflies in a jar that don't give light enough

You kept on a dresser and stayed up, and yet
They wouldn't glow all that night
When we went for a visit

Vaida Keleras, photo: *At the winter solstice, Lithuania, 2016*

WINTERLY

To walk the snow-bleached streets
squinting back tears
and almost hear my ears
squirm to a burn
by a steeled shield
glazing sun-bright yellow
urine diluted to yolk

Strong wind rounds each corner
with a two-punch too late
for me to duck I lean
into a crouch and keep
both fists scrunched deep
inside my pockets

Each step offbeat
to advance lame
foot forward in
retarded prance

I can only be in Chicago
where a highrise sprawl
quiets the whistling
along the grit-free
streets I walk

Take a walk today
along the parkway
and stop to pick up
a fallen leaf that's still green

A sparrow on the turf nearby
chirps to say "they'll turn
all the way" and you want to
believe him and look up to see
the tree stripped now only has
shadow left underlining
each striving limb

       *

For the faith you have
in small things will not
aggregate into one sum
the next big thing after
you've run the course
will stay shorn of next
to nonsense clearly
a no brainer

       *

Take Mayakovsky he
would not have wanted
the oversized statue of him
put up to overlook the plaza
with no word left for him to say

But how that could stop a live or
surviving passerby in the traffic
swarm a revived and thriving
world revolution with so
many random gunshots

Our filmed serials cannot
hold or contain so much

ANON, FOR TONY LONG

Daylight bright as gold
makes everything shine
to the full score of ten

Chirping birds and bugs
are all out directing
the springtime renewal

Daytime so bright
carries the light
into every nook

Let the fret disappear
from everywhere
even here

Daytime has no end
while I think of my friend
lost for too many years

Two years younger he was
and now he's gone
I have to catch up

He introduced me to wine
while I urged him to read
beyond the school's precedents

We ate rich dark
rye bread from his
grandfather's bakery

And traded quips
on both being misfits
with no clear career aims

But shoulder to shoulder
we'd go far and for years
wrote letters each day

To discern and convey
what the world had in store
while we were so far away

To expand the measure
from each place we stayed
I could only treasure

His Bavarian parlays while
my own lack of movement
brought on a dark dismay

I'd only learned to mock
my friend's thriving getaways
but he was giving in the least

And brought back gifts to please
such a relay we lived by
of essential fundamentals

Lines from and for Viktor Shklovsky

"Everyone kept his coat on but Mayakovsky,
who removed his to boost morale."

21 sept 07

I've kept a marker to this page since 1973, when I first came across it. I was no younger then, just young enough to know the difference between a smile and its historical antidote; some may not vouch for it, but I know there is such a thing. At best, if you can believe, it's a musical whirligig, like the Valkyries Ride, strung out in the strings, meshing and blending, while the trombones coax a melody till the sopranos come screaming in. And where does that leave us?

12 nov 05

Alya, just why can't you leave me alone? Alya
I feel I can speak with you, openly, since I feel
I've known you, Alya, you are never the same, say
What I will, what I feel, all-knowing, or at least
Wise as Solomon, your counselor even, Alya
Allow me to digress about the hem of your dress
While my mind strays and meanders back to
Your hair, its fringes sparking and looped, so
Tightly charged into a bond of febrile intensity

Nostalgia is snow where it sprouts
Green to the eyes as the innocent pasture in
Giorgione's gnomic perspective on the true
Source of our current estate, prehistoric though
We're apt to call it, if not mythic, where the
Wildness has been tamed enough to contain
A modest apologia

Nothing if not enough
And the sky was falling, as it still does, for
Chicken Little, if he hasn't had a change of mind
And our future will hold nothing as extraordinary
As a revelation, not to cancel even the least
incremental measure
His or her story like a surge
out of the prehistoric luster, fog-enshrouded as
a loud precipitous cloud, in a state of being there, not
a whit more or less, the bald apprehension of a suspended
moment, as absolute as a winding sheet, tight as swaddling
to correct an observed splay-foot trend, which never did
become popular, never rose to surpass any standard, or
measure at heart we kept and cherished, each signal to
the heart a searchlight swept up in each casual outward
glance, taking in the territory at large, mundane details
notwithstanding
Love stories aren't always what
they're cracked up to be, not always lively in the track
of their development, nor centered to hold interest in
the crux or ordeal of arousal   All while fate has a
fixed date with its future

THE GREAT UNLOADING, FOR COMRADE BORIS

Vague quadrants of light right on the unwashed
piers scrubbing that goes on under

History now a hardline mess a hard time
those who made it dying to make a comeback
the American way like Nixon
who's to catch the blame no one but ourselves

There's a body shop REBUILT RESEALED   next
                                        to the bus stop
a disabused bench where the old guys sit just a
                                vacant stare away
while a van with dark-tinted windows like a tennis
    blister throbbing I WANT YOUR SEX inches
into the intersection on a delayed red

    "The Shadows are Back" a sign-painter reads
the graffitti aloud & his colleage, wielding bucket
& brush like top hat & cane in a black & white
Fred Astaire routine (now in white & black) steps
up to "give the matter my personal attention"

Match This

Too early to tell, while it clearly shows, there's a seminal
Glow to every corner, and not just from the displaced furniture

Polish, remover of choice, chip embellisher, put in trust
And nicely too, is there no telephone, here either?

Hurry to tell the time, a Beckett rhapsody, bold standstill
Environs where you can't not blend in, even unto

Perpetuity, the arched avenue of elms venting itself, where they
Knew Polyphemus stuck a rose up his ass, but couldn't even catch

Call for you must be by pre-arrangement, in your modest chambers
No visitors allowed, house rule

This worry is too sad, the whiteness of the wall is indistinct
With waterstains off-color in a pose struck en vogue

Except for tomorrow, life would stop right now
It was no dream, but this is

CLOSET CHRISTIAN

Turning the black & white pages till they blur
Into newspapers on the days after a small-scale
Blizzard and before the sanitation dept goes out
On strike or the sun shuffles in and raises all manner
Of uncoordinated riot no one ordinary day can contain

Don't bother to turn the statistics acrostic
Neither will the key fit nor is the turnout predictable
Just unleash the animal magnetism from your eyelashes
Toys that bump their lumps till the eyeballs fall out
Will not let me pick up after them in sheer amazement
Though I know to keep all the latest gizmos in my brain
No amount of overexposure will get me to return
To the factory where they follow a manual

It's premature to turn back while I keep Sunday in my heart

As of 11/12/13

When you wake to see snow
        swirling with late-flown leaves
                in a whirling descent

the blurred trail of their slant
        may say where we went
                but not that I want

you to stay with me
        charmed as I am
                by heart's warmth

FOR EGG SAMPLE

A mother at sea
        finds it hard to see
her son is inclined
        to hold to the wind
clouds too astounding
        the waves beat in
with cannon fire at war
        west of here
the sky grows dim
        seared by the sun
wind bites in
        to feast on winter
gnawing on what
        it can't find
later at dusk
        the moon rolls in
while a trimmed sunlight
        keeps wailing
the late-hour call to prayer
        simmers down
singed it flew off
        the tongue
my high sign
        a stunned goat

Thanks to Luisa 6-26-92

it's not the happiest time but your call cheered me, thanks
a lot, did you go to lots of birthday parties as a girl, come
to think of it I never did, maybe twice that I

remember wearing the fancy hat with elastic strap
like a stiff joke on de rigueur

Suicide catches everyone short, surviving friends want the least
thing to hang on to, even a casual acquaintance on getting it
second-hand like me has a fear of being sucked in by the ripples

I forgot to ask also what you got to read

Am in awe of what must be your daily confrontations with the ocean
it's so elemental, reviving the sense of smell, it's where people
go to get pink & pickled, weekends for a fine bronze & brine

I spent my best childhood days one summer on the shore of

One of the world's minor waterways, but it was all of sun & salt to me
the bay at Flensburg, on the Baltic, I was nine then, so
I remember watching sunsets as late as nine p.m. being

impressed by the fact of staying up late as the daylight.

Bug Mechanic 3/17/92

When words begin to "enfold" the silence
Curl up on themselves into blank nostalgia
Or rigorous brown studies
Escaped from the night past starlit margins
Like crayons stepped on and crushed without being
Drained of their true color
In a garage abandoned overnight
Where the wornout axle no longer hums
And rags soak up on atmosphere
An uncapped grease-gun lapses into a lasting
Commentary with every durable thing
Outliving its rust in retired obsolescence

Count on observance of a general
Hollow-eyed desolation
Before an upstart of the last retort prepares a relapse
As solid an anchor for the next fading day as silence

AMTRAK ADVENTURE

Hi: you look like the conductor for this train
I have a young gentleman here, eager to make it through
to New York City, ETA: he's just had a full
breakfast, even been to the bathroom, so he's ready

To see the country, what there is of it, etc
so of course, you'd like to be invited too

But first, let's reseat ourselves and pretend we have pillows
and then maybe we'll know which way the wind out there blows
sooner than we make change, we'll ring some changes way before
the desolate depot where we disembark admits to daylight

ADD-ON PLUS

Take a minimum of sense
Then split it in two it's
Love what you get
No wisdom in view

Now you know no reason
Much better than this
To unscroll kept secrets
Just to energize bliss

And envision the charm
How your countering kiss
Sets off an alarm
I don't dare to resist

So we're lucky to share
Such pleasure as this

Summer: Go Slow

Glass cracks, and the rats get busy
Smoke climbs where you cannot reach
To patch a hole up in the sky

And so it's time to pound the streets, trash any squawking
Brilliant cars we find wanting, snap their locks
Storekeepers crash their gates to and rush away to tamer
Suburban firesides

Catch a lurid glow from the cool evening news
Those dreadlocks of sundown
Siren-heaved scorchings

Everything is justified but the law
Which takes back the Samaritan cloak
To reveal a quivering specimen

By what right the police are too quick to tattoo
A verdict with their nightsticks

The sun scorches everything

A local reservist breaks into his action camouflage
And double-times it to the station
Overnight bag in one hand and rifle in the other

How can you even believe
It was Nielsen's Summer Symphony
Got us through that winter

*

Not if I screamed the snipers were out to get me
Or a shortage of bread snuffs dreams if it's true
In both forecast and affliction retrograde be damned
O Sir, God help me, no!

*

No not another election campaign
This tower of bullshit has two eyes and if you believe the guy
It couldn't be worse you're seeing right through and from
But with no hope of getting out

Raw Pedigree, For Sanjay Agnihotri

Your eyes see into the future
Beyond days and years
With no kind of feature
Precisely defined

The chance of a blunder
Is always nearby
If only to let you defend
What terror's awakened

No friends can mend
Though all involved
Should plead reckless cause
No party will aim for remorse

For sure all knowledge is local
So far as you get to go by

                    *

Wild birds will sing
                    their springtime
To bring in summer
                    if one takes the lead
The rest join in
                a chorus
With flowers
                while a radiant
Sunrise begins
                to sink in
And warm
                the bright-lit
Coast of NJ

Restricting the Sonnet

when shall I tell you where I haven't been
grass doesn't grow there either

get the questions right next time
right!

you never ever do time
right?

she said with a vengeance with flair
with a builtin vow

first there was there was
then I would begin

now we're homing in on the sky
its hollow valley deepens

a turnabout crushed velvet black
glass crystal stains rehearsed

FROM EARLIER DATES IN THE ANNALS

Before it even started, the world was in a mess (they'll say
again and again, as though it mattered); you lie down and
the moment passes into something medial or

[undated]

as to the way it happens, just follow the tracks
mildew's overgrown, if not swept away, a fragrant array
from early disposal of disavowed remnants deleted
THAT of the last it could be said aptly to apply :
Wet as summer rain's inspection of a specimen mudpie
Of, viz.,

HOW MANY DAYS OF YOUR LIFE HAVE YOU BEEN ALIVE?
asks the man in the foreground of the group taped and photographed
for the occasion

20 Aug 07

when the shadow gets dis place   J   I
sum o' things, nothin's to be done   E   L

the new splurge
a washout from the snorkel emission
clouded the waters with waves never mind
their color

Terminal 4

the ceiling arches on reflected light (on)
a motionless Calder mobile (unmoving)
a preflight apprehension rises, raises
a subtle human stench (all too human)
        3 nov 03 JFK 5:30 pm

More from
If & when
I should meet you in the street
Shadow & web of my lost arteries
If & then
It should happen that I see you
I'm unable to come up with your name
And think of you later, though not as
Before, but deranged, dipped in the fire of some outlandish misconception
Misconstrued, misfired strategies on a guitar, boldly overplayed, snapped
Clean & vanished, no more wind to strum
Merely "look, chum: No hands, the fingers licked clean away"
Way a cat crouches to gnaw & jaw-grind
Dripping gristle to marrow, off an end-bone, so its nearer eyelid
Quivers into decompression
The songs we never made, our curiosity keen yet curiously
Unempowered
Vacancies of Easter windows greeting the sunrise
Arias of suspense from a high-rise
High-strung on a high C
But if you turn the page
There's still room for a poem, enamored of labyrinths,
Frivolous myths, the raw plumage of frottage, shortbreath
Screaming, keen dolor left unimagined, all wet in a reclusive afterglow,

Burnt-cylinder bedfellows,

Sneers & rants, the regrets that follow empurpled passion, brazen & loony

Honeymooners, our celebrity-duo once blissed out, then

Outdistanced the magnetic drones of flashing paparazzi to a blind desert,

And in a stupor of far-out hilarity and festal

Inebriation finally did, after repeated tries lasting

Past midnight, plug the one-eyed lamppost guarding a six-pack

Arizona gas-stop, right in the socket, right where they were hauled in,

Booked & glossed for the tabloids

("Cut!")

But by a marvelous ingenuity, quantum desire cut a road through

Burma, never mired down in Vietnam, punctured eardrums cued a bedroom

Generation, downplayed the humdrum, replayed on celluloid

Romantic retreads amid lumpen retreats, rolling in postluvial

Mud at the base of neoclassical poise to a swell of unmuted

Strings, roiling & tremulous, its two-timing counterpart

Under a tin dome, waist-deep in regrets, stalled

In the inner workings

(cut!)

Smashed

in the

Mirrors

time couldn't erase its worst feature

while each day offers the same excuse

Mother stands there sad and grieving

with no time since Time is grating

nanoseconds from our meeting

You should know the face I'm wearing
bears your traces in the morning
even as the night is nearing

I no longer know the meaning
caring for a chosen clearing
in the mirror when I'm shaving

There's no future within hearing
fear one outlook that I'm sharing
with no mole endured the swear-in

Partial Rondelay
I stayed put and waited
but you were not where I wanted
what with your own dream to pursue

So close to touch was the feeling
your voice alone made real even
the legend I kept on believing

When by trial our trust broke in two
intuition kept up its appeal although
the loss was more than I could feel

Now that you are gone I know
there's no tomorrow I know of
is even worth waiting for

Your hand in mine all too real
for my oppressive appeal

There's a man with a cardboard house on his back
I walk up to him and ask where he plans to spend
the night. It's nighttime already he tells me
then looks me straight in the eye to say it's
all right you don't want to know everything.

                    Day 2 into his Age of Reason
                    June 17 has the young boy raging:
                                                    "You're not
                                            boss of the whole
                                        world & I don't
                                        have to do anything
                                    you say"

            Fear glints reflected in the nasty eye
Here comes
                    Hoppety-lopetting, low-slung & bulbous
Slim paws
                    Long-fingered, exposed to the raw concrete
Sidewalk
            winter has depopulated

            Let me tell you about the night
Instead
            by the emblematic dream that came of it

The place I remember
    the wild wave struck before we could rally against it
    so even losing count of the few of us there all before
    we could think to prepare were survivors might possibly
    since we had our minds swept and no moment set to say
    goodbye or the time

no longer aware

what could you or I dare

the house no longer standing

a mudhole wipeout

though unbeknownst the sky helps
somewhat to widen the highway

long before the woods the words fill their way in

starving for air
    for the loose ribbon your hair makes

so whoever would dare to claim you
        would have to rename you

around Stonehenge
a round of stones
was found there
to resound
like
    nowhere
            else
before or since
except the Mayans
had it written into
their priestly code

for their pageant
was meant to dazzle
their uninitiated workforce

Slow chronic calendar drift that
day's worn-down shoes come off
abiding a hairshirt one day has
a live skunk's living cell, when
it's come to that now it's all the
smell we talk about having no other

And among my (snowbound) animal friends
I have none as intimate or chatty as the Rat

                laughs, barely able to suppress
                the quiver in his elegant whiskers
                    whenever I speak
                of coming down to his level
he lets me know just how welcome I am
                  I plan to stay
unwashed, till I take on his coloring plus coat of grime
keen-eyed, with a rapid sniggering grin moreover
by wind-thrashed moonlight
              6-22-82 On sunny side of the
a.m. street a Chinatown kid hunkers down magnifying glass in
hand aiming to ignite a full glaring sheet of newsprint spread
out before him on the sidewalk; a wisp of smoke lifts from
the soft mole of a bronze scorch-mark that darkens and buckles
before a blaze erupts
              "field-optical"
Bent on hazard, the high risk implicit, sand-grains chafing,
              water-lapped
11:30 p.m. 7-6-91   Drinking late in bars – how did we

even get here?
What say 's a
name?

      "sky bait tv; ai?"
scrambled, back from lower Australia; or
some sidereal (say) Iberian
bent via shortwave:

                      ai-ai-ai

      Don't tempt me,
Birdsong

                      'taint Brahms
But it goes with the leaf-green, hidebound
Ivy to give mortar pause, ant-wise

                        and what was that
Dream all about, in winter, wild overbearing burden
      Of things to reconsider, a density of involution in
A chokehold had weeds & grasses enthralled, ancient
In the brickwork, hid inside its chinks & sinkholes
though starved through, unto sickness
's not enough ("I-I-I") arise as if
only to go, and every time seems
a woman always there to save Him

timpani & trombones slugging it out
"like fate"   cruisin' for a bruisin'   insisting on
      "an arc of raised eyebrows"
no less
      now there's more where that came from   What's this
needs more
      insider reading & filler

As per Liszt

Clear manipulation fires up a spectacle for each ear.
No key gets lost, so they cut loose
Just at imtermish. I shd hv been w/latecomers,
AntiB brigade, Bach & early Brahms, though
Boring to miss these first 2
So file in, refueled
Fireworks come next to carve into the silence
Some blast that piece, when played well lasts 1 hr
A cobbler at the piano piercing & hammering,
Transformed to a forging clangor superbly controlled
Beyond the pretense of technique really becoming transcendent
Done live rousing trills

Retro Fit
From struttin' in the mirrors
and jammin' in the park
I've grown a bit recessive
it's no longer just a lark
the future's now pure fandom
my love just hit the bank
the rest long lost in levity
just counting on my swank

Professional I've never been
my manager recruits me for
what late-blown trends alert me to
ambition falling flat
I'm never going back
to where I'm never home
the reasons are the real ones
and I'm ready to sign on

From shadow into sunshine
the days sure creep along
if I don't keep my soul elastic
I'll never know what's wrong
and groan until the world growls back
and the new day shan't begin
till lightning's flogs the night away
I'm ready to pitch in

No need for hesitation
no lesson will be lost
we're simply not a nation
you can forfeit at one toss
if the president keeps signing
with a leaky fountain pen
both gain and loss will turn chaos
so we can't find our feet again

New millennium is a dinosaur turning the corner, much of the world may be holding its breath for a clinching prophecy to come true. Poets are the ones will address what's to be said without yielding to the abrogation of hindsight. Poets, it is to be hoped, will work like ardent archeologists to reclaim the past, even while the groundwork shows no yield, recondite. Still, once poetry does surface, it's more than a lightning-glint breaking into the future. The day will be there, full-blown, but it will call for some spirit to adapt, for the eyes to sustain the steady light, and more than a grain of humor. Luckily for us, dear reader, all that is just what we have in store.

Total Focus
If I had the whole world in focus
with a term for each changing spin blurring by
a lasting trumpet blast to sound the SOS
whenever rage flicks off its handle like an axe

If I had time to solidify the anger
and lisp the consequences like a tarpaper wasp
when the noon heat strikes its quiet hammer
or grinds a blind despair with every mote

If I had time and kept a climbing score
to keep a world of difference from my door
while raw need unfurls a jaundiced flag

And the flood did not sport the test of a dime
to stand still or still stand there
a country can lose its heart in uncensored ruin

Disclosure likely for the average human span
                    an arching design with drumroll punctuation
headlong with conniptions into corruption
                    NorthGerman over the Viennese
                    (inbred rather than acquired)

Limp as the leaves
                    Nothing in mind
                                        Except wind
Say it's not
absurd, this farting at the margins of sense
from an icy wind; plus the lashing sting
in rejection for each attempted gasp
the would-be survivor insists on

                    But did I never mention to you the insomnia
                    time weaves in, out of reality
                    like a crazy weathervane, whirring

as the skiff had veered dangerously off, having
cleared harbor, made free of heaving reef-bound
breakers, then swept cargoless, skimming out to sea

with the last point sighted, without the least
resistance, cracks without creaking, seamless
as a voice from the dead interim, unimposing

for a code beyond cracking
the desert rid of shadows
by flickering mirrors
unimaginable: unsayable

mere elements,
without the complement of weather.

WHENEVER

When you dream of someone
all so far away you'd never
hear the voice she spoke in
though her image stays

It's how I think of Nanno
in a blur of golden light
the shimmer of pure day
I cannot hold on to

Delights are few where memory
lands if somehow out of reach
some particulars though continue
to teach and guide us to pursue

Nanno's name the banner
that bright early morning

AFTERTHOUGHT

Age piles up the memories
To bulk like shoreline debris
After a shipwreck. Where
The waste shows in a tidal slur
I've rolled up my sleeves
To sort remnants. So I stay put,
Familiar with a load of sludge,
And place the names and faces
Of those I knew. Not all of them
Are dead, though even those
I stay in touch with seem remote.
Even when we meet, we go over
Most of our own forays that seem
To have little in common. Most
Days slide by that way too.

Elegie, for Tony Long

Our world
Holds up a see-through mirror with
Daytime merely a cover for blackness
Which is sure to come back once
You don't show grief is what
Shows up in everything

Until
there is no escape as matters would have it
In the way the plot of a noir intensifies to a rapt
Focus: betrayal or the quick shift in a friend's
Unreciprocated side-glance reticence O if only I'd
Known of a way to pursue

The sheer shock
Or aftereffect curtailed each time
It gets shorted you get jogged awake and then what

An unengaging environment like a landscape that
Persists in keeping its distance

If I cannot it's because you're not
Anywhere to be seen.

Where you entered
Unknowing
A field of flame

Inside the yellow-brick vault
Behind some wall they ground you
Down to fine particles a pallid retreat

White weightless ash hovering
Across the lawn and the roses
Straight from the florist their stems

Leaning as from a wind-tossed wreck

The music your friend
Steve Lacy's soprano sax
Wailed made us
Look up to the sky

And so I rushed to write
Our mutual friend Lou
"8 widows showed up
For Tony's memorial"

Long gone
You were
Even when
Comatose

When I came to
View your corpse
It was still remains
Unspeakable

The pain it was
To look you over
Not real enough

When I flew
To get there

What could I
Have said to you if
Words would find a way

Our days together were a spin
Fraternal doubletalk
We didn't always hear

Tears flow to say
You are awake
Despite the pain

Comatose tears
Down your stilled
Cheeks flowed still

But even if you had
Managed to come to

Would we have
Known each other

In the way young
Tolstoy came to
Test himself

Jump up from
The floor from
Supine position
Unassisted

Attempted mentor
That I was when
You were sixteen

Brothers Karamazov
I said was the
Book to read

And so you'd read
More Dostoyevsky
Even before

You learned
To read the
Russian

And then the music
The flute you played
In classical trios

From sheet music
I never learned
How to read

There was the time
You took me for
A car ride so far

And long it got
Me out of my
Depression

Over the girl
Friend I'd lost
For good

I don't recall
I ever got to
Thank you

Another time
One evening
We were down
At the stop

Waiting for a bus or
Train to Cambridge
Just the two of us

And a pretty young
Woman you said
You couldn't make
A move to greet her

I told you to think
What you'd feel like if
You failed to proceed

You approached her then
Went off and spent
The night together

Though I didn't take
My own advice
The regrets piled up
To this day

"At the start
of this volume
I'm alone"

From this the first
Entry in your fecund
Journals of the new
Casanova of 1969
And on to 1972

By then the scroll
So many affairs
Scoring no trend

To secure insomnia
The ego has to hustle
And find a respite

"Furious love
twas too, good
as it should be"

RECOMPENCE

Quick as the getaway was
I could not hold you
Long enough in my arms
So longing pains a broken heart

Our lips sealed the contract
I thought could never break
Such an illusion we'd believe
Until it turns too late

The clock I can hear ticking
Outpaces my urgent pulse
If I outlive a century
I'll not catch you not once

RETROGRADE

Your hand so small it was hard to grasp
Soft as your voice to say it couldn't last
Though every side-glance stayed sparkling

A pearl in each eye the tears had dried
To the voice that vouched reassurance

Incrementally as new life begins I tremble
In its early stages while love is more
An abstract condition such distress
Where passion has been and is gone

A cold embrace won't take me very far
Now desire strikes spikes instead of sparks
By the strict rule death has imposed
We'll stay apart I'll learn to mourn

And stay alone where I have never been

The Overlook at Monte Grappa

(12 Jun 11)

The stars, once so compelling, stare us down
I mean it's night, here on this ferocious bald boulder
Of a mountain, where children run on a flattened path
Mild moonlight holds them wrapped in ribbons of mist
Hidden as the hills below, even the wide ribbon a river
Where it runs off down the Alps clear as a sunlit sky
Is lost in the mystery of night with the municipal
Sanctions to the numerous executed upstarts of '44.

So now I am nearly ready to meet the future
With my time clocked in no face is harder set
No place secured more exclusively out of eleven
Bronze plaques the rain has defaced to look like
Tombstones with mugshots in Soviet cemeteries
Calked in cement to always look fresh after rain
Or, as in a cemetery, through tears.

HELLO

As the foreword
prior to any beginning
is a primal essay in pursuit
of the new hope for equal
affection or friendship
before the possible bond
is put to the test of enduring

What's real is ahead in each
unrealized sanction of refined
hesitation without any notion
of either alliance or for a broader
network of allegiance just as if only
a smile could verify securely what is
the plain truth of a minor disclosure

As the man is supposed to have said
on his way to the scaffold
one never knows just where it's best
to rest one's head
so as to make each step you take
count for an advantage
given its unforeseeable
unconscious advance

If we have shade to shield us from
a parched scorching sunstroke
beyond any relief that praying
for a tolerable end before
the coming day unreels smug from
a nighttime of somnolent relief

Tomorrow is as good as goodbye
once the sorrows weigh in

No Recourse

If there's no sure way without street signs
or tracks to mark the trail then intuition
likewise shows no guidelines to avoid guilt
meanwhile it's too early to joke too early
and yet the immediate future still holds
a dread just ahead measured in incremental
instances without at all being foreshadowed
and wisdom will always stay a gainsay only
after the fact is revealed to be true

So long as we don't question what to say
stays an enigma the least hearsay may
fail to give flawless clues beforehand

Words of esteem have no face value
baseless as a flooded basement
so unexpected in advance no claim
to assess loss of stored lifelong
valuables you'd come to count on

Before you know how much it means
fate fashioned an eager toil ahead
of disaster or the very next
breath you take

When trees in the woods snap
and crackle with no wind you feel
you're in too deep to avoid snakebite
or a hunter's set snare in the leafage
a right before cuts loose so beware

THE WOUND

even if it's to the heart will heal
without showing a scar much like
spring flowers after the height
of their late-summer crisis
will fade to embrace the fall

HÖLDERLIN: TO THE FATES

from the German

Grant just one summer, you that have the power,
And one fall for my song to ripen,
So my heart be more inclined, once it's fed
Up being toyed with, to die on me.

Without coming into its divine right while alive
A soul drowned in Death can get no rest there either.
But once all that's holy and close
To my heart works out in the poem,

Come on then, stillness of the shadow world, I am
Content, though the strings I played
Not go with me on my way out, that one time
I did live like the Gods and want nothing else.

Orion's

tears of streaked acid rain on the window I look out of today
mean money all means inflation may be melting no matter
the upkeep what widened wings can shelter us from
the streaming imprint of starlight or sunshine to reclaim so
that's how our money is minted a firm foundation all basis
cash each sandal you shed on your black pilgrimage
in a steep struggle to keep from reverting once more
apologia into a perpetuated nostalgia

Acknowledgments

With grateful appreciation to Benjamin Sloan, editor of the eminent past journal *Mothers of Mud*, where several of these poems first appeared.

With much gratitude also to Steve Luttrell, editor of *The Café Review*, in which a good number of the later poems were first published; and to Walter Robinson also, who posted one on Instagram.

Thanks as well, and as usual, to William Benton for his vibrant friendship along with unusual editorial savvy.

And last but not least to Kimberly Lyons, with my love for her loving care.

Front cover: M. K. Čiurlionis, Tempera on paper *Prelude,* 62cm x 73cm, from the diptych *Prelude and Fugue,* 1908; by courtesy of its permanent storage within the M. K. Čiurlionis House in Vilnius, Lithuania.

The painted images herewith contend in greater detail with the originals.

VYT BAKAITIS is the author of *Deliberate Proof* (Lunar Chandelier Press, NYC). *City Country* was his first book (Black Thistle Press, NYC, 1991). He has also published translations of poetry from several languages, with his versions of the classic Romantics Hölderlin and Mickiewicz included in *World Poetry* (W. W. Norton, 1998). Two books of his translations from the Lithuanian poet Jonas Mekas have appeared: *Daybooks 1970-1972* (Portable Press at Yo-Yo Labs, NYC, 2003), *There Is No Ithaca* (Black Thistle, 1996) in 2018, *Words Apart and Others* (Brooklyn Rail Editions), and most recently, his own poems appeared in *Refuge & Occasion* (Station Hill Press). Bakaitis also edited a volume of essays by poets on Jonas Mekas's poetry, *Message Ahead* (Brooklyn Rail Editions).

www.ingramcontent.com/pod-product-compliance
Lightning Source LLC
Chambersburg PA
CBHW030915140626
46545CB00017B/2371